MASTER YOUR MIND

HOW TO CALM YOUR EMOTIONS, MANAGE STRESS, REDUCE ANXIETY AND FIND YOURSELF

TABLE OF CONTENTS

THE PURPOSE OF THIS BOOK

If you've spent your whole life searching for a certain kind of emotion, this book will help you find your way to it.

The following is a guide for reading this book.
Instead of reading this book to gain knowledge, try to gain understanding. True wisdom (or insight) comes from inside. Insight comes from seeing inward, hence the name. Everything you need to know about life is already stored within you; all you have to do is learn how to access it. Your inner self is where you'll find the solutions. This book is meant to point you in the proper direction. I appreciate anyone who can keep believing that the thing they need is still out there. Hope has been restored. You being here, reading this, is evidence of your faith, courage, and strength; without hope, we have nothing. If you keep going in the direction you are and keep holding onto the hope you have, you will find what you are seeking for.

I must stress that this is not the only book with truthful information. The truth can be found anywhere and in anything. The truth (the spiritual) can only be seen and experienced by going beyond the appearance (the physical). The book's contents are not to be taken as gospel. They are an indication of the truth itself. You must look deeper than words to find the truth. The only way to know the truth is to live it. Since the truth is ineffable, there is no way to put it into words.

Truth can be found by going beyond words and into the realm of emotion.
Many people who find out the truth say they feel an overwhelming sense of joy, love, and calm. It's been called the "most familiar unfamiliar feeling" by those who have experienced it. You've arrived at your true home. If you can identify that emotion,

you can unlock any secret. Nothing I write in this book will contradict what you already know to be true in your heart. That's why the moment you finally see the truth will seem so strangely familiar.

Don't waste your time trying to solve it logically, because you won't. As soon as you try to analyze it logically, you lose sight of the point. Truth cannot be gained by learning a few sentences by heart. A child can accomplish it, but they won't grasp the reality of the situation. The truth manifests as an emotion. The answers you seek, the truths that will set you free, will emerge from that emotion. That's the holy grail we're all after, right?

What I reveal in this book will seem elementary at first. Your brain (ego) will battle against it or try to make it more complex since it will appear almost too simple. It will suspect that nothing could be easier than this. In that moment, keep in mind that the truth is always uncomplicated. Anything that seems complicated may be simplified into its component elements. What makes anything true is that it cannot be dissected into its component parts. This is why there is a simplicity to the truth. Seek simplification if you really want to know what's going on.

If you read this book with an inquiring mind and a sincere desire to learn the truth, you will find the answers you've been seeking.

Before we go any further, I just wanted to say how much I appreciate you taking the time to be here and listen to me out. Thank you for bestowing upon me a portion of the most potent vital energies you possess, by doing so you are doing the same for yourself. Keep in mind that it is only because of our divinity that we are human.

Chapter One

FREEDOM FROM SUFFERING

Do you dislike what you are doing right now? A part of you may be doing it because it's your job or because you decided to do it and are actually doing it. Are you harboring an unspoken grudge towards someone close to you? Are you aware that the energy you are emitting has such negative affects that you are actually polluting both yourself and those around you? Give the inside a good look. Does anything even remotely like resentment or unwillingness exist? If so, pay attention to it on both a mental and an emotional level. What images is your mind forming of this circumstance? Next, consider your emotions, which are your body's response to those thoughts. Feel the feelings. Is it a nice or bad feeling? Do you genuinely want to own this energy inside of you? Have you got a choice?

It doesn't matter if you are being taken advantage of, your current activity is monotonous, someone near to you is untrustworthy, annoying, or unaware. It doesn't matter whether your feelings and ideas regarding this circumstance are justified or not. You are in fact fighting against what already is. You are turning the present into your adversary. You are causing dissatisfaction and internal and external turmoil. Your misery is contaminating not only the people around you and your own inner self, but also the entire human race, of which you are an integral part. The contamination of the world is merely an external mirror of an inner psychic pollution caused by the negligence of millions of unknowing people toward their own inner lives.

Stop what you're doing, talk to the person in question, and express your feelings fully, or stop focusing on the negative aspects of the scenario that your mind has constructed and that serve no useful function other than to reinforce a false sense of self. Understanding its futility is crucial. Negativity is never the best response to any circumstance. In most circumstances, it really keeps you there, preventing actual change. Anything done with negative energy will pick up its contamination and eventually cause additional suffering and sorrow. Additionally, any unfavorable internal state can spread: A physical illness is harder to spread than unhappiness. It generates and feeds latent negativity in others through the law of resonance, unless they are immune, that is, very cognizant.

Are you contaminating the world or removing the trash? Nobody else is in charge of your inner space, just as you are in charge of the globe. Humans will stop producing outside pollution if they are able to clean up their own inner pollution.

THE ROOT CAUSE

When discussing pain, it's crucial to distinguish between two separate states. In this work, I refer to mental and emotional anguish simply as "suffering." There is a technique to avoid mental and emotional anguish no matter what challenges you face in life.

I am not implying that the difficulties we face are figments of our imagination. Daily, people suffer terrible losses and setbacks. What I mean is that even though we all feel pain, suffering is not necessary. The point is that while we can't stop bad things from happening to us, we can control how much suffering we put ourselves through.

When anything bad happens to us, Buddhists believe that two arrows are shot in our direction. Getting hit in the body by an arrow hurts. Experiencing emotional agony (suffering) twice is unbearable.

The Buddha once said, "We don't always get to shoot the first arrow in life. Our response to the first arrow is shown by the second. The second arrow might be be omitted.

A few years ago, when I first heard this remark from Buddha, I was baffled because I knew what he meant but couldn't figure out how to apply it to my own life. I seriously doubt that anyone in their right mind would choose to suffer if given the explicit option of suffering or not suffering.

Just deciding to avoid pain seems impossible. I seriously doubt that anyone would still be in pain if that were the case. I wasn't able to put an end to my pain until I learned a new perspective on its origins, and that didn't happen for a long time.

As I began my quest for personal development, I was exposed to a wide variety of philosophies, scientific investigations, and therapeutic practices. I tried waking up at 4 a.m., changing my diet, becoming more structured and disciplined, engaging in shadow work, learning about different personality types, meditating every day, attending spiritual retreats, following spiritual masters, and studying various ancient religions.

Name it, and I've probably experimented with it. I was determined to find the solution because I wanted to alleviate my own pain and that of others.

Some of these items helped me get better, but they didn't eliminate my pain entirely. Every day, I still felt a tremendous amount of anxiety, worry, unfulfillment, irritation, anger, frustration, and heaviness. The truth is that after all that, I was even more confused than before I began this quest since I still hadn't found the answer.

I had no idea what to do with my life and felt completely lost. I had no idea what to do, where to turn, or who to ask for help from. It wasn't until I was at my lowest point that I saw a tiny flicker of light at the end of the tunnel.

The answer to my own pain was suddenly revealed to me by one of my first mentors, the person who trained me to become a coach, after I had spent years searching for it.

Understanding how our minds function and how the human experience is fabricated led me to the solution.

THE DIFFERENT WORLD'S

We live in a world of thought, not reality. Giordano Bruno said, "It's not matter that generates thought, it's thought that generates matter."

People's perspectives on the world can vary widely, even across those who are physically close to one another. One could be having a quarter-life existential crisis in a coffee shop, worrying uncontrollably that they have no idea what they're doing with their lives while it seems like everyone else has it all together, while the person sitting next to them is calmly sipping their freshly brewed drink and watching the world go by. You and your friend are in the same coffee shop, sharing the same air with the same strangers, but your perceptions of the world could not be more dissimilar. We can all be present at the same moment and place, and yet each of us can have a vastly different experience of it.

Another proof that we inhabit a mental realm rather than a physical one. How many different replies do you think you'll get if you walk up to a hundred strangers and ask each of them what money means to them? Almost a hundred distinct solutions! Although we all use currency, it has distinct connotations for different people. Money can be good or bad; it can buy leisure, freedom, opportunity, security, and peace of mind, or it can be the impetus for criminal activity. I won't go into detail on which is correct at this time (hint: there is no correct answer; more on that in a later chapter).

Here's another case in point that exemplifies this idea: How many different opinions do you think you'll get if you poll a hundred people and ask them what they think of our current president?

Most individuals are so wrapped up in their own thoughts and interpretations of the world that we might ask a hundred people the same question and receive a hundred different replies, even if we are talking about the same person. How we feel about something is determined by the significance (or thinking) we attribute to it. That interpretation or line of thought becomes the lens through which we view the world; as a result, we experience life through a representation of reality rather than reality itself. The fact is that the occurrence occurred, with no room for speculation, analysis, or interpretation.

It is up to us to build our own reality based on whatever interpretation we give to the occurrence. This is how we construct our individual realities. What makes us feel good or horrible about something is not what happens to us, but how we choose to perceive those occurrences. In this way, those living in the developed world can be more miserable than those in the developing world, and those living in the developing world can be happier than those in the developed world. Emotions are the result of internal processing rather than exposure to external stimuli. The only way to know what we're thinking is to experience it.

Suppose, for the sake of argument, that you despise your job and that it is a major source of worry and annoyance for you. You hate going to work, and the mere thought of doing your job gets you angry. You could be relaxing on the couch with your loved ones while all of you are thinking about how frustrated you are with your job. Except for you, everybody seems to be having a great time.

Even though the same thing is happening right now, everyone in your family is experiencing it very differently. The mere anticipation of going to work altered your vision of the world even though you weren't actually there. If it were true that exterior events lead us to feel the way we feel on the inside, then you would be ecstatic to sit in your living room and watch a comedic TV show with your loved ones every single time.

Now, you might object that you're only feeling this way because your job is a stressful and anxiety-inducing factor in your life. If that's the case, then I have to ask: is it true that everyone has the same feelings about their job? Even if two people are performing the same tasks, they may have vastly different experiences due to individual differences. One person's idea of heaven on earth is another's idea of a living hell, and vice versa. In the end, how one feels about their profession has nothing to do with anything other than their own thoughts about it.

Let's revert back to the fictitious situation where you despise your job. Keep in mind the feelings of worry, fear, and anger that just thinking about it brings up.

Let's take a mental exercise and try to figure this out by responding to the question below.

Without the notion that you detested your work, who would you be? Don't go any farther until you've taken a minute to think about it and see what comes up. You will probably feel and be happy, calm, free, and light if you refrain from overthinking it and actually let the answers to surface from within you, without that idea. When we remove the filter of our regular thoughts, our perception of an event or object changes dramatically. We build our own reality, starting with our own thoughts, and thus, we live in a world of thought rather than actuality. You have now, with this insight, found the root of all human emotional anguish...

Our own way of thinking is what ultimately causes us pain.

I'm not arguing that we're imagining things, so please don't toss this book across the room and set it on fire just yet. The world as we see it is extremely real. What we believe will be felt, and what we feel will be real. That can't possibly be disputed. But until we see how our reality is constructed, our thoughts will appear to be fixed in stone. Since we can only ever feel what we are thinking, altering our emotions is as simple as altering our thought processes. Knowing that our thoughts create our reality empowers us to alter that reality. And if that's the case, then achieving a condition of no thought is always just a thought away, and it can completely alter our life in an instant.

In a nutshell, the beginning of our joy occurs when we stop thinking.

You will probably feel and be happy, calm, free, and light if you refrain from over-thinking it and actually let the answers to surface from within you, without that idea.

HOW CAN WE STOP BEING NEGATIVE?

By letting it go. How do you put a hot coal you are holding in your hand on the ground? How do you get rid of some unnecessary and heavy baggage you are carrying? by accepting that you don't want to experience the discomfort or bear the weight any longer, and then letting go of it.

Deep unconsciousness, like the pain-body, or other forms of deep pain, like the loss of a loved one, typically require transformation via acceptance and the light of your presence — your focused attention — over time. On the other hand, if you realize that you have a choice and are not just a collection of conditioned reflexes, you may easily let go of many patterns of regular unconsciousness that you no longer need or want. All of this suggests that you have access to the power of Now. You are without options without it.

Chapter Two

THE NATURE OF THOUGHTS

THE FUNCTION OF THE MIND

Because it was essential to our survival, human beings evolved to become capable of complex levels of reasoning, analysis, and thought. The human brain performs a fantastic job of keeping us alive, but it doesn't exactly set us up for success. It cares just about making sure we don't die, not if we're happy or fulfilled while doing so.

The function of the mind is to warn us of threats to our safety in the physical world. It's so good at what it does that it not only monitors our immediate surroundings for risks, but also draws off our accumulated knowledge base to imagine what-if scenarios and make predictions about what it thinks could be future possible dangers based on our memories.

Nothing about this is even remotely incorrect. Simply said, the mind is operating as intended. We'll get mad and annoyed with it when we can't accept that all it has to do is ensure our survival. All arguments stem from naive miscommunication.

Survival is the mind's primary responsibility. The job of our minds is to make us happy. The search for inner contentment, love, and joy is the very reason for your journey.

Because we no longer live in the wild where danger lurks behind every bush, you can release your mind from its duty. It has done an outstanding job at its intended function. The mind interprets every stimulus as an attack on our basic survival, so as long as we rely on it, we'll feel perpetually threatened, anxious, fearful, frustrated, depressed, angry, resentful, and so on. If you want to be liberated, joyful, calm, and overflowing with love, you must stop relying on your rational mind alone and instead tune into something bigger that will ensure your survival and flourishing.

WHERE DOES REALITY ORIGINATE?

All of reality is built from the mental and energetic raw materials of our thoughts. Nothing can be felt without a corresponding thinking. Realize that thinking is a noun, not a verb, and that thoughts are not something we produce but rather something we possess. We don't have to do anything to have an idea; it just happens. Similarly, we have no say over the random thoughts that enter our heads. Something outside of our brains, call it the cosmos if you like, is where ideas come from.

On the other hand, thinking consists of reflecting on our own mental processes. It requires a lot of work and determination, both of which are limited resources. Thinking entails consciously interacting with one's internal mental processes. Thinking occurs when you give some attention to a notion rather than ignoring it.

All of our emotional and mental problems may be traced back to our thinking. At this point, you may be asking how optimistic outlooks factor in. Feel-good thoughts, or positive ideas, do not originate in the mind. Peace, love, and joy instead arise from who we truly are. They result from one's actual existence rather than one's thoughts. In the following chapter, we'll discuss this topic in further detail.

For the time being, let's engage in a brief mental exercise.

I'll pose a question, and all you have to do to answer it is pay attention to what's going on right now; we can go over the results later.

How much do you hope to earn annually in your ideal world?

Put the brakes on for a moment and see if an answer appears.

Take 30 to 60 seconds to come up with a number that represents your ideal annual income.

Do not proceed unless you have developed a substantial line of reasoning around the amount of money you wish to acquire.

Multiply that figure by five now.

Is a fivefold increase in your income, as a new aspirational target, acceptable to you?

Spend at least 30-60 seconds more contemplating your reaction to that thought and what else comes to mind as you let yourself feel your emotions.

Do not proceed until the foregoing has been completed.

Come back in, let's go over what happened.

A number flashed into your head within seconds of my initial question, "What is the dream amount of money you want to be making per year?" One could think of that. Take note of how easily and fast something occurred to you.

I then asked you to give some thought to the response that had just occurred to you. What happened after I prompted you to deliberate on a response?

Once you started thinking about it, your emotions undoubtedly soared through the roof.

Perhaps you've been telling yourself that you'll never be able to make that much money, that nobody in your family ever has, that you have no idea how to generate that much money, that it's stupid to desire that much money, or that doing so will make you greedy.

Pay attention to how you felt during those mental musings.

I'll show you what to do about it soon, but I imagine it didn't feel great.

This is a classic case of thinking against thinking.

If I ask you a question, without fail, an idea will immediately occur to you.

THE NATURE OF THOUGHT IS NEUTRAL.

Keep in mind that they are the creative raw materials of our minds.

When we start to reflect on our thoughts, our emotions start to swing wildly. When we reflect on our own thoughts, we often find ourselves judging and criticizing those thoughts and experiencing a wide range of negative emotions as a result.

You considered a number when I asked how much money you were hoping to earn. That was an unaffected, non-emotional thought. You may have even felt elated and unconstrained. The uncertainty, unworthiness, fear, wrath, guilt, or any other emotion you may have experienced first surfaced when you considered how much money you wanted to make.

This is what I mean when I say that our thoughts are the source of all of our pain. Until you started thinking about your thoughts, just the mere idea of how much money you wanted to make didn't hurt.

There's no need to analyze or criticize our internal mental processes. Doing so would serve no useful purpose. Even though our minds trick us into thinking it's helping, it actually only makes us feel bad about ourselves and come up with excuses for why we shouldn't want something or why we can't accomplish something.

The only thing that was helpful and beneficial was your first response to my question about salary expectations. Everything that went through people's minds after that was harmful and counterproductive.

What we think about becomes real. Thoughts are destructive.

There are endless reasons why we can't do it and why we can't have it, but the moment we start thinking about the thoughts, we immediately project our own limiting beliefs, judgements, criticisms, training, and conditioning onto the notion.

By bypassing conscious processing, we ensure that no preconceived notions of failure or failure to achieve one's goals will cloud the purity of the original idea.

If I were to ask you how you would go about making the amount of money you desire, suggestions would begin to form in your mind if you sat and thought about it for long enough.

These are the seeds of original ideation. Minds are limitless, boundless, and full of good energy. Having thoughts from the divine will make you feel good, lighter, and more alive.

You'll be hit with a barrage of negative feelings, including heaviness, restriction, and limitation, as soon as you start contemplating the ways you can make the money you want. This is how you may test your level of consciousness.

When I want to know if I'm receiving cosmic thought downloads or just thinking about thinking, I check in with how I'm feeling.

Since thoughts can never be seen, feelings and emotions serve as a kind of intuitive internal dashboard telling me whether or not I'm thinking too much.

I know I'm thinking too much if I'm experiencing a lot of negative feelings. Another way in which our biology favors our achieving our goals.

This is what I mean when I say that our thoughts are the source of all of our pain. Until you started thinking about your thoughts, just the mere idea of how much money you wanted to make didn't hurt.

Chapter Three

FREEING YOURSELF FROM YOUR MIND

OUR INNER DIALOGUE

Most usually, a patient who complains to their doctor, "I hear a voice in my head," would be referred to a psychiatrist. The truth is that, in a manner very similar to this, almost everyone constantly hears a voice or voices in their head: these are the uncontrollable mental processes that you are unaware of your ability to control. chats or monologues that never end.

You have probably seen "mad" persons on the street who babble or mutter to themselves constantly. The only difference between that and what you and all other "normal" people do is that you don't say it aloud. The voice offers opinions, makes judgments, compares, grumbles, expresses preferences, and so forth. The voice may be revisiting the recent or distant past, practicing or anticipating potential future events; it is not always related to the situation you are in at the moment. Worry is when something frequently imagines something going wrong and having a negative effect. This soundtrack may occasionally be accompanied by pictures or "mental movies." The voice will interpret it in terms of the past even though it is pertinent to the current circumstance. This is due to the fact that the voice is a product of your conditioned mind, which is a product of both your individual and collective cultural mind-sets. As a result, you observe and evaluate the present through the lens of the past, which completely distorts your perception of it. It happens frequently for people to be their own worst enemies. Many people have an inner tormentor who haunts them constantly, punishes them, and saps their strength. It is the root of countless instances of suffering and unhappiness as well as sickness.

OBSERVE THE THINKER

The first step can be taken right now. Start hearing your inner voice as often as you can. Pay close attention to any recurring ideas, such as those out-of-date phonograph records that have been playing in your thoughts for a long time. This is what I mean when I refer to "watching the thinker," which is another way of saying to pay attention to the voice inside your head and act as a witness.

Be objective in your listening to that voice. Don't judge anyone, in other words. Because doing so would indicate that the same voice has entered again through the back door, refrain from judging or condemning what you hear. You'll quickly realize that the voice is there, and that I am hearing and seeing it. This revelation that I exist and this awareness of my own presence are not thoughts. It originates outside of the mind.

As a result, when you listen to a thought, you are conscious of both the thought itself and of yourself as the thought's witness. There is now another level of con-sciousness. You sense a conscious presence—your inner self—behind or, as it were, underneath the notion when you pay attention to it. Because you are no longer supplying the mind with energy by identifying with it, the thought then loses its hold over you and swiftly dissipates. This is the beginning of the end for compulsive and unconscious thought.

You feel a break in your brain stream as an idea fades away, or a moment of "no-mind." The gaps will initially be brief—a few seconds maybe—but over time they will lengthen. You experience a certain stillness and peace inside of you during these pauses. The peace and silence will get stronger with repetition. In actuality, the depth of it is infinite. The delight of Being, a subtle outpouring of bliss from deep within, will also be felt.

It's not like being in a trance. In no way. There is no loss of awareness in this situation. The situation is the contrary. Both would be worthless if the cost of tranquility was a lowering of your consciousness and the cost of stillness was a lack of vitality and alertness. You are far more awake and alert in this state of inner connection than you are in the mind-identified state. You're entirely in the moment. Additionally, it increases the energy field's vibrational frequency, which sustains the physical body.

You become aware of the condition of pure consciousness as you delve farther into this area of "no-mind," as it is frequently referred to in the East. In that condition, you are so intensely and joyfully aware of your own presence that all thought, all emotions, your physical body, and the entirety of the outside world seem comparatively inconsequential in comparison. And yet, this is a selfless state rather than a selfish one. It pushes you past the boundaries of who you previously considered to be "yourself." That presence is both fundamentally you and incomparably greater than you. There may be a paradox or even a contradiction in what I am trying to say here, but there is no other way to put it.

By focusing your attention on the Now, rather than "watching the thinker," you might interrupt the flow of thought. Just focus on being fully here right now. It is quite satisfying to do this. By doing this, you are able to detach consciousness from mental activity and enter a state of intense awareness and alertness without thinking. The core of meditation is this.

You may put this into effect by giving any ordinary task that is typically only a means to an end your whole focus, making it become an end in and of itself. Pay special attention to each step, each movement, even your breathing, while you ascend and descend the stairs in your home or place of employment, for instance. Stay fully present. Alternately, when washing your hands, focus on every sense experience connected to the task: the sound and feel of the water, how your hands move, the aroma of the soap, etc. Alternatively, after entering your car and closing the door, take a moment to stop and pay attention to how your breath is moving. Become conscious of a subtle yet potent presence. The level of inner calm you experience is a reliable metric by which you can gauge your progress in this practice.

So learning to disidentify from your mind is the single most important step you can take on your path to enlightenment. The light of your consciousness gets brighter each time you stop the flow of thought.

One day, you might find yourself grinning at the voice in your head the way you would at a child's antics. This implies that since your sense of self does not depend on the contents of your intellect, you no longer take it seriously.

DO WE NEED TO THINK POSITEVELY TO FEEL THAT WAY IF WE CAN ONLY FEEL WHAT WE THINK?

The idea that we can only feel what we're thinking has a limitation that I haven't yet discussed. To put it more accurately, we can only ever experience bad feelings when we are thinking.

The point isn't necessarily to never feel anxiety, stress, fear and sadness again. Fear, for example, can be a useful emotion to have before venturing down a dark alley with no one else around.

Some of the negative feelings, such as fear while choosing to walk alone down a dark alley with no one else in sight, might be beneficial. These bad feelings are only beneficial to us in terms of surviving, but for the majority of us, if we don't frequently face life-or-death circumstances, negative emotions are more detrimental than beneficial.

We'll proceed under the assumption that we're not fighting for our lives on a bodily level, in which case we'll assume that most of the time negative feelings are unnecessary.

Most people assume that we must think positively in order to experience pleasant feelings when I suggest that we can only ever feel what we're thinking.

Let's conduct another thought experiment so you may discover the truth for yourself rather than trying to persuade you that something is true or not. Think back to a point in your life when you had the greatest amount of joy and love, and try to feel those emotions as strongly as you can for at least 30 seconds.

When you felt the most love and joy, what kinds of thoughts were going through your head at that very moment? What ideas were going through your head at that precise moment is what I'm asking, not what you were doing at the time.

When answering this question, a lot of people come to the realization that they had no thoughts at that very moment. Others claim that the thought was one of extreme happiness or gratitude.

For those who said they were grateful, did you experience that happiness and love before or after having that thought?

Spend ten to fifteen seconds responding to that query before moving on. What realizations and insights did you have?

What's astonishing is that most people didn't think anything when they experienced the highest levels of happiness and love in their life. Those who expressed gratitude in their thoughts felt that way even before they did.

If they had that thinking, it would have come after they had experienced those emotions, therefore the thought could not have caused the emotion.

This leads to a second truth: you don't need to think or have thoughts in order to experience joy.

Truth is beautiful because it can be experienced right now and does not require justification. The experiment we just conducted gave you direct experience with this truth, therefore you don't need to be convinced of it or given a good reason for it.

Here's why we don't need thinking or thought processes to experience joy and love.

Joy, love, pleasure, liberation, and thankfulness are the states in which we are naturally. Why don't we always feel that way, if it's natural, may make this difficult to accept. I'll respond to this shortly.

Looking at nature and the state of anything while it is young (before it is influenced and conditioned by its environment) is one of the best ways to view something in its natural state.

Take a look at a baby in its unaltered state as an illustration. What is a baby's normal state, presuming the child hasn't been maltreated, mistreated, or suffered from any health problems? Are tension, anxiety, dread, and self-consciousness innate in infants? Or do they already exist in a blissful, joyful, and loving state?

Joy, love, and tranquility are aspects of who we are by nature. Since thinking will always pull us away from these natural states of being, it seems sense that whenever we experience acute stress, we are thinking A LOT. The intensity of the bad mood we experience directly correlates with the amount of thinking we are engaged in at the time.

On the other side, the amount of thinking we are doing at any given time has an inverse relationship with how strongly we feel a pleasant emotion. In other words, the joyful mood we experience in the present is stronger the less thinking we are doing.

Consider a few such instances in which you can clearly see how much thought was being done at the time and you will realize that this is true.

Spend a minute or two doing this.

Then look back to a couple moments when you felt the happiest or most joyous and in love, and assess how much thinking was going on at those moments.

Spend an additional 1-2 minutes doing this before continuing so that you may truly comprehend and digest the truth of what you see.

My coach used the analogy of our mind having a speedometer (like in a car), but instead of miles per hour, it is ideas per minute to help me understand this notion. The "thought-o-meter" rises the more thinking we do, and if there is enough thinking going on, it enters the danger zone. At this point, we experience great tension, exhaustion, frustration, and anger.

The fact that we are thinking at all is what stresses us out, not what we are thinking. The amount of tension and unpleasant emotions we are feeling at any particular time are closely associated with the quantity of thinking we are doing. Just remember that you're thinking when you feel a lot of annoyance, tension, anxiety, or any other bad feelings, and that the intensity of those emotions is directly proportional to how much thinking is taking place.

<u>Therefore, misery is caused by what we are thinking, not WHAT we are thinking about.</u>

In conclusion, we do not need to "think positive" in order to feel love, pleasure, ecstasy, or any other positive emotions we desire because experiencing those feelings is part of who we are. Only when we start thinking about the thoughts we're thinking, which blocks the direct link to Infinite Intelligence, do we not naturally experience these emotions. Instead, we experience tension, anxiety, depression, and dread. Our sorrow is mostly brought on by the fact that we are thinking, not the content of our thoughts. The quantity of thinking we are doing right now and the strength of our unpleasant feelings are directly related. The more space we create for happy feelings to organically appear, the less thinking we do.

Chapter Four

HOW HUMAN EXPERIENCE IS FORMED: THE BIG THREE

These three concepts—Universal Mind, Consciousness, and Thought—are the essential building blocks of the human experience. These three guiding principles enable us to fully experience whatever we do in life; if any one of them were absent, we would be unable to engage in any activity. Sydney Banks was the first to discover these ideas, and now I have the honor of imparting them to you.

Knowing how to use these three principles not only enables us to produce from Source but also to know how to relieve our own suffering.

UNIVERSAL MIND

All living things are controlled by Universal Mind. It is the vitality and energy present in everything. The planets' ability to maintain their orbits, the ability of an acorn to grow into a tree, and the ability of human bodies to repair injuries are all examples of this. It's how our bodies are able to maintain themselves and keep us alive without our active participation in bodily functions like breathing and heartbeat. The Universal Mind is the name for the intelligence that is capable of doing all of this and is present in everything. Numerous names for this entity exist, including God, Infinite Intelligence, the Quantum Field, Source, and others. The source of all things in the universe, including thoughts, is here. The Universal Mind connects everything. There is no difference between anything, and each time it appears that there is, it is just our minds playing tricks on us. We experience a sense of completeness, fulfillment, love, joy, peace, and inspiration when we are in touch with the Universal Mind. The only time we stop this flow of Universal Mind and start to feel distant, irritated, lonely, angry, resentful, sad, frightened, and afraid is when we start thinking (believing the illusion or ego).

UNIVERSAL CONSCIUSNESS

The collective consciousness of everything is known as universal consciousness. It is what enables us to be conscious of our thoughts and conscious of our existence. We wouldn't be able to have any experiences without Universal Consciousness. There wouldn't be anything to employ our five senses for, thus they would be useless. It is this that gives things life and allows us to perceive them.

UNIVERSAL THOUGHT

The foundation of the universe, from which we can construct, is universal thought. It is our capacity to think and give the universal mind's energy form.

It is the thing our consciousness allows us to perceive. We wouldn't be able to be aware of anything without thought. The DVD that contains all the information necessary for us to watch a movie on the TV is analogous to thought. The TV and DVD player are analogous to consciousness in that they give us a way to watch and interact with movies by bringing the information on the DVD to life. In the same way that Universal Mind is the intangible energy/force that unites and powers everything, electricity, which is required to power the DVD player and TV, is analogous to that. It is the Origin from which all things flow and operate.

Chapter Five

HOW DO WE STOP THINKING IF THINKING IS WHAT MAKES US SUFFER?

DON'T SEEK YOUR SELF IN THE MIND

On a mental level, problems with the mind cannot be resolved. There isn't really much more to study or comprehend after you have a basic understanding of the disorder. Similar to how studying crazy is insufficient to produce sanity, studying the inner workings of the mind may help you become a skilled psychologist, but it won't help you get beyond the mind. You already know the fundamental workings of the unconscious state: identification with the mind, which develops an ego-based false self in place of your authentic self, which is centered in Being. You essentially turn into a "branch cut off from the vine," as Jesus describes it.

The ego has unending needs. It lives in a condition of anxiety and want because it feels exposed and endangered. Once you understand how the fundamental malfunction functions, you no longer need to investigate all of its numerous forms or turn it into a challenging personal issue. Of course, the ego enjoys that. It will readily attach itself to your troubles since it is constantly looking for something to attach itself to in order to maintain and reinforce its mistaken sense of self. This explains why a significant portion of so many people's sense of self is closely tied to their issues. The last thing they want after this has occurred is to be rid of them because doing so would mean losing their sense of identity. Unconscious ego investments in misery and pain can be very strong.

Therefore, you can exit unconsciousness once you realize that it is caused by identification with the mind, which naturally includes the emotions. You become conscious. When you are in the moment, you can let your mind be without becoming caught up in it. The intellect is not defective in and of itself.

It is an excellent tool. When you look for your identity in it and take it to be who you are, dysfunction sets in. After that, it transforms into the egoic mind and rules your entire life.

LET THE THOUGHTS PASS

Since it's impossible to just stop thinking, the most we can do is limit our mental activity so that it decreases gradually over time. Eventually, we can reach a point where we spend the vast majority of our days in a state of joyful contentment, unencumbered by our thoughts.

Many people think we mean we want to put an end to all thought when we declare we want to stop thinking. This isn't the intention behind our actions. Now that you understand the distinction between thoughts and thinking, you can focus on practicing letting thoughts come and go without overanalyzing them.

The most intriguing and perhaps paradoxical aspect of halting our thinking is that we need do nothing more than become aware of it in order to reduce it. Realizing that our thoughts are the source of our pain helps us become self-aware and emotionally detached from them so that we can let them subside and pass on their own. This may be accomplished with minimal exertion simply by being fully present in the moment.

One of my teachers gave me an analogy that perfectly explains this idea:

Picture I've handed you a bowl of muddy, foggy water to drink. How would you clear the water if I asked you to do it?

You have 15 seconds to think of a solution and move on.

The common responses involve either filtering or boiling the water. The dirt in the water will begin to settle on its own after some time has passed, and the water will clear up on its own, but most people don't discover this until it's too late.

This is also how our thoughts operate. Let your thoughts settle down on their own and your mind will be free of pondering if you don't try to "filter" or "boil" them. If we don't mess with it, our minds are as transparent as water in their natural form.

When your thoughts stir up the dirt, clouding your mind, and making it hard to see ahead, you can now attribute these feelings of confusion, disorganization, and tension to something external. You can take this as a sign that your mind is wandering and you need to stop thinking so much.

Understanding that our feelings are merely reflections of our thoughts and that our thoughts are the source of our distress helps us to view things as they really are. Then we give it time and space to settle, and we discover that we are gradually regaining mental clarity.

Thinking is like sinking in quicksand, too. When we try to suppress our unpleasant thoughts and feelings, they just get stronger. It's the same with quicksand. We can't fight our way out of quicksand. If we get scared and try to battle it in a frantic manner, it will just increase its hold on us and drag us down more quickly. The only road to freedom is to give up the fight and let your body's natural buoyancy carry you back to the surface. The only way out of our mental prison is to let go and have faith that our innate wisdom will lead us back to sanity and tranquility just as it has in the past.

Know that it's quite natural to go through phases of thinking and not thinking. Trying to achieve a state of non-thinking 24 hours a day is an impossible objective that will only lead to mental anguish when we give in to temptation and start thinking again.

While our spiritual selves are unlimited, our bodily bodies are not. Because of this, we will inevitably experience both anxious/stressed and joyful/peaceful emotions, since we are a literal living bridge between the human and the divine. The mind's natural ebb and flow between thinking and not thinking is something we have little control over, but we can learn to spend less time thinking and more time experiencing positive emotions.

It may seem like a curse to be unable to choose when our minds start to think, but this is not cause for alarm because we can always revert back to a state of non-thinking. It's all a part of being human, and it's a beautiful thing.

Knowing that this condition of pure peace, love, and fulfillment is always present beneath any thinking we may have at any given moment is what can give us actual peace. That ideal state is not something we can attain or lose; rather, it is something we may forget. However, our ability to disregard it does not mean it does not exist. Even though we can't see it during the day, we know that the sun rises and sets every day. When the sun goes down, it's only natural to feel some trepidation and worry if we believe it may never rise again. The same holds true for how we currently feel.

It only takes a moment of awareness to tap into an endless supply of wisdom, love, joy, peace, and fulfillment. Sometimes we forget, but when we do, and we recognize that we are trapped in our thinking while we are feeling down, that knowledge alone is enough to bring us back to our natural, beautiful state. Remembering that the sun will rise again soon is all that is required to put our minds at ease and move on with our lives. With such knowledge in hand, we may appreciate the nighttime for what it is and what it contributes to the cosmos as a whole. We can begin to appreciate its splendor on par with the sun if we realize that it is intended to be a part of our human experience.

Chapter Six

HOW CAN WE SUCCED WITHOUT THINKING?

THE MOMENT OF ENLIGHTENMENT

Here is a query that will help you think more deeply about this concern:

What ideas are running through your mind while you're working at your most best and completely engrossed in what you're doing right now?

Wait for a response to appear for roughly 15 seconds before continuing.

Here's another query that can help you if you still haven't experienced the illumination or revelation from the response:

What ideas are running through your head right now when you're in the state of flow, which is when you're love what you do so much and are so immersed in it that you lose all sense of time and space (also known as when you're in a state of pure flow)?

Wait a moment (approximately 30 to 60 seconds) for the solution to emerge before continuing.

You aren't thinking right now when you're producing your finest work and are completely in the zone, when there is no distinction between you and the work you're performing. And if you are thinking, it just comes to you naturally without your having to think about it. In other words, the state of non-thinking can be used to define human performance at its highest level. We operate best when we aren't thinking, despite the fact that this may sound absurd, as you just experienced.

Here is another illustration to further demonstrate the validity of this statement. Do you believe that professional or even Olympic athletes overthink and analyze every single event that takes place during a match? What sort of thinking do you suppose is occurring while they are competing? The best athletes will say that they are in "the zone" when they are performing at their absolute best. This "zone" is also known as the "flow state" or "non-thinking state."

IN THE STILLNESS OF YOUR PRESENCE, BEAUTY EMERGES

Satori is a term used by Zen teachers to describe a moment of entire present, no-mind, and insight. Be thankful when satori occurs because it provides you a taste of enlightenment even though it is not a long-lasting transformation. You may have in fact gone through it repeatedly without understanding what it was or how significant it was. To recognize the splendor, majesty, and holiness of nature, one must be present. Have you ever been astounded by the utter silence and unfathomable size of space as you stared up into the stars on a clear night? Have you really paid attention to the sound of a forest-dwelling mountain stream? Or to a blackbird's singing on a calm summer evening near dusk?

The mind needs to be still in order to become conscious of such things. You must temporarily set aside all of your knowledge as well as your personal difficulties from the past and the future; otherwise, you would see but not see and hear but not hear. You must be fully present.

There is more to this than just the beauty of the outward forms; there is something that cannot be named, something indescribable, some innermost, most holy essence. This underlying essence emerges in some way whenever and everywhere there is beauty. Only when you are there does it open up to you. Is it possible that both your presence and this unnamed essence are one and the same? Without your presence, would it still be there? Go into it thoroughly. Take a look for yourself.

You most likely were unaware that you briefly fell into a condition of no-mind when you had those experiences of presence. This is because there was a too-narrow chasm between that state and the onslaught of thought. Even if your satori was short-lived before the mind entered, it was present because you would not have been able to appreciate the beauty without it. Beauty cannot be created or recognized by the mind. That beauty or that sacredness was there only for a brief period of time while you were fully there. You were probably unable to recognize the essential distinction between the perception, the thoughtless awareness of beauty, and the identifying and interpreting of it as thought because of the narrowness of that gap and your own lack of attentiveness and alertness: Because of the brief pause in time, it appeared to be a single process. In actuality, though, all you possessed at the time it first entered your mind was a remembrance of it.

The deeper you are as a person, which translates to mean that you are more conscious, the longer the pause between perception and cognition.

The beauty of nature does not truly exist for many people because they are so mentally imprisoned. It's only a mechanical mental classification when they say, "What a pretty flower," for example. They cannot genuinely see the flower, feel its essence, or sense its holiness because they are not still and present, just as they cannot truly know themselves, feel their own essence, or sense their own holiness.

With very few exceptions, modern art, architecture, music, and literature lack intrinsic beauty and substance since we live in such a mind-dominated culture. The explanation is that folks who produce those things are unable to break free of their minds for even a brief period of time. As a result, they never experience the inner space where creativity and beauty are born. Monstrosities are produced by the intellect when it is left to itself, and not just in art galleries. Take a look at the urban settings and industrial wasteland we have. There has never been such evil produced by a society.

Chapter Seven

IS IT RIGHT TO SET GOALS, HAVE DREAMS AND NEW HOPES?

THE PRIMORDIAL SOURCE

I was bouncing up and down, excited, relieved, and grateful when I finally realized that thinking was the source of all of my misery. I had found the real cause of every bad thing that had ever happened to me. This bliss, however, was fleeting because as soon as the excitement subsided, the following questions entered my head: If thinking is the source of all my misery and I cease thinking, how do I spend my life now? What about all of my objectives, aspirations, and dreams? Do my wants in life eventually go away? Will I eventually become a couch potato and stop doing anything with my life?

I can read your mind, in case you were wondering, and I am telepathic. Just kidding, but if you're wondering how I came up with the exact or very similar questions and knew what you were probably thinking, it's because, contrary to common perception, I am also a human. You may be sure that many individuals are experiencing the exact same feelings as you are as you begin to realize your genuine grandeur because we are all on similar awakening journeys to our genuine Selves.

Returning to the original query, what should we do with our ambitions, dreams, and goals if we cease thinking? Because I believed that I would have to give it all up and become a monk in the middle of the mountains, I started to feel an amazing amount of fear and anxiety as I thought about these questions. Undoubtedly, I wasn't prepared to do it. Even though a big portion of my life was characterized by misery, I actually enjoyed being in the world and sharing the fullness of life with other people. However, I wish I were that enlightened and separated from my existence.

Here is what I've learned, using this new knowledge, on what to do with our objectives and dreams. There is a distinction between thoughts and thinking, as we have previously mentioned in prior chapters. There are differences between the source of thoughts and the source of thinking, and the source will determine whether a thought creates misery or not.

Similar to this, the source of our objectives and desires will impact whether or not we feel wonderful about achieving them. There is nothing fundamentally good or terrible about anything in this world; our perception of it creates that reality. It's not really an either-or situation because goals, desires, and ambitions are neither good nor evil; rather, the question is where those goals are coming from.

TWO DIFFERENT LENS SOURCES

Goals might come from two different places: from inspiration or from a desperate need.

We have a strong sensation of scarcity and urgency when goals are set in a state of desperation. We may even feel intimidated by the enormous responsibility we have just taken on. It feels heavy and burdensome, and we start to experience imposter syndrome and self-doubt. We also constantly feel as though we don't have enough time for everything. We run through life hastily, looking outside of ourselves for solutions and methods to reach where we want to go faster. We never feel like we have enough or that we can ever obtain enough. Worst of all, even if we succeed in achieving our objective, those same sensations of lack quickly return hours or days later. We start out without satisfaction in our work, unable to enjoy our successes, and because nothing we do ever feels like it's enough, we experience the same feelings about ourselves. Without knowing what else to do, we search about for external guidance by observing what others are doing and discovering that they are still engaging in the same behavior. So, in a desperate attempt to stop the negative emotions from eating away at our soul, we go ahead and create another goal. When we look a little more at the goals we set, we find that they are usually "means goals" rather than "end goals." Therefore, the objectives we create for ourselves in this desperate situation are all just means to an end. We always have a reason for wanting to reach the objective, and that reason always has something else in mind. For instance, we can want to start a multimillion dollar company because we desire financial independence or we might want to leave our work to avoid the stress and worry that comes with it. Instead of wanting to do these things, we feel as though we HAVE to. Goals developed out of desperation are usually "realistic" and based on past experience as well as what we perceive to be "plausible" at the time. It is extremely restricting and restrictive. When we first strive to make these kinds of goals and aspirations come true, we sense a lack and an urgent need to fulfill the dream, despite the fact that they may first delight us. Ironically, if we succeed in obtaining a desperate aim, we experience even greater emptiness than before. The next "logical" step is to create a goal that is even more ambitious, driven by an even greater need to feel complete on the inside.

Most of us set our goals and conduct our lives in this manner. Additionally, I'm not saying this to condemn or pass judgment, but to lay bare the truth. Only because that was my life was I able to explain it in such agonizing and awful detail.

The good news is that there is a way out if you set goals in that manner; it is not your fault. It involves setting objectives and desires that are motivated rather than desperate.

It's a whole other story when we set goals out of inspiration rather than desperation. We are producing in this mode because we are profoundly affected, inspired, and expanded. Rather than feeling like a duty, it feels like a calling. It seems as though there is a strong life force within us that yearns to be articulated through us and materialized into the physical world. For this reason, even if they never get paid or are able to support themselves doing it, artists create art, dancers move, authors create, and singers sing. We get a strong urge to produce something. We draw closer to it. We are obligated to carry it out. When we experience this, we are acting from a place of abundance rather than scarcity when we create.

The most shocking thing is that we are currently creating for no other reason than our own pleasure. We don't make things because we feel compelled to. There is no other reason why we create; we just do it because we want to. We are not setting these goals in order to accomplish something else or as a way of obtaining something else we desire. This generating originates from a position of wealth and wholeness. It is brimming over with love and joy for life. The majority of us want or have children for this reason. It's not so we can take advantage of our children once they are old enough to work and utilize them, hopefully, as a retirement fund. We want to have children because we want to share our abundance with them; this comes from a position of giving rather than expecting something in return.

Because it is not of this world, this profound inspiration is exceedingly difficult to convey. In reality, it comes from something higher than us via us rather than from us directly. The thoughts and vision we have for what we want to create seem to be much bigger than we could ever have envisioned or come up with on our own, which is why I prefer to refer to this feeling as divine inspiration. Divine inspiration doesn't evaluate or rely on past evidence or what you or anyone else in the world has already achieved because it doesn't originate from us but from someone bigger. When ground-breaking breakthroughs and ideas are made that, not too long ago, appeared impossible, divine inspiration occurs. It is not constrained by any limitations or bounds. We feel energized and lifted by this enormously expansive force, which gives us a "high" from life. In this state, we experience wholeness, completion, and an abundance of unfailing love, joy, and calm. We genuinely live, love, share, give, create, grow, and nourish ourselves rather than analyzing, contrasting, criticizing, or justifying anything. The ability to experience the divine as humans is undoubtedly one of the finest experiences we can have, and this is possible since we are all descended from the same source.

Everyone has felt the burning urge to make a positive contribution to the world out of pure inspiration rather than out of necessity. I urge you to test this notion before reading the next sentence. Take a moment to pause and consider instances in your life when you were compelled to produce something extraordinary because you felt profoundly inspired and called to do so. Think of a time when you had the need to produce something out of inspiration. It doesn't matter if you actually did so or not.

Isn't that one of the most incredible feelings there is? Most of us experience this heavenly inspiration, but as soon as we start to consider acting on it, we repress it. We start to doubt ourselves, make excuses for why we can't do it, convince ourselves that it's unreasonable, that we should put more priority on other things, and that we're not capable of doing it. As soon as we start to consider the idea of wanting to create, the source of that inspiration is completely cut off, and we resume living our regular lives. When we shut off that source, we also cut off the emotions of abundance, ecstasy, joy, and pure unconditional love and return to the emotions of doubt, anxiety, frustration, and despair. We also feel constrained, stuck, and frustrated with our existence.

We can never pursue more than one calling at once, whether it is inspiration or, in the here and now, desperation. The two cannot coexist simultaneously, but we can alternate between them based on how much thinking is going on at any given time.

We really revert to our true nature and start to generate goals and aspirations out of inspiration rather than desperation when we stop thinking. We don't cease having goals and dreams when we stop thinking. We start to make room in our minds for universal ideas that give us the heavenly inspiration to do something that has never been produced before. We experience a sense of aliveness, wholeness, joy, love, peace, and fulfillment when we heed divine inspiration.

How therefore can we determine whether a desire or aim was born of inspiration or desperation?

Simply remembering the difference between thoughts and thinking can allow you to determine whether a goal or dream is the result of inspiration. Inspiration is the source of all goals and desires that manifest as thoughts. Thinking-based goals and desires are made out of desperation.

In order to develop our new goals, we frequently analyze, assess, critique, justify, and use our past experiences. However, this method feels incredibly constricting and limited. Since these goals are being pursued out of desperation, we often don't feel good when setting them or while working toward them.

Observing your energetic state is another approach to differentiate between the two. Desperately set goals and dreams will feel incredibly weighty, draining, confined, and empty. We frequently experience feelings of shortage, dread, and worry, as if we are required to do it. With these kinds of objectives, it seems as though failing to achieve them will have serious repercussions, which adds to the pressure and stakes (I'm sure you can now understand how this might lead to the feeling of desperation). Furthermore, we believe that we are pursuing these objectives in an effort to leave our existing circumstances and escape from something. Most of the time, when we set objectives in this stage, we do so with the intention of doing something else later. For example, one of our goals might be to quit our work. You'll probably have this objective since you want to move on to something you genuinely enjoy doing, but it's clear that quitting your work is really simply a means to an end. Or perhaps you've set a goal of making $1 million because you want to be financially independent and explore the world. Always a means to an end rather than the end itself, these objectives. We always have a reason for wanting to achieve these goals, and failing to do so leaves us feeling quite hollow on the inside.

I want to underline that none of these objectives are intrinsically undesirable or that we shouldn't have financial success or employment independence as objectives. That is totally different if those objectives were conceived as a result of inspiration. Just the source of the goals matters, not necessarily the goals themselves. Making this distinction is crucial; otherwise, you'll waste most of your time worrying and fussing about whether or not this is the correct objective for you.

There are only objectives that are set out of inspiration or desperation; there are no right or wrong goals. It just depends on how you want to feel on the inside. Once you are aware of these two sorts of objectives and how they come to pass, you will be able to feel euphoric as you set out to make fantastic things happen in your life.

Goals and ambitions that are the result of inspiration, on the other hand, feel incredibly light, invigorating, uplifting, and expanding. We frequently experience delight, excitement, and most significantly, inspiration. Although we don't feel compelled to produce it, we DO want to. You feel motivated to accomplish it rather than feeling like you HAVE to. Since we are not aiming to escape anything or our existing circumstance by achieving this goal, there is essentially no pressure. We don't feel as though we are creating from a position of shortage or urgency; rather, we feel as though we are creating from a place of abundance and we just want to share it with the world. Since it is a spontaneous act, we are not doing it to obtain something from it so that we can carry out another task. It is merely an end in and of itself rather than a means to an end. There is no need for us to invent a "reason" for it. We don't create in order to feel complete; rather, we create because we feel complete and want to contribute from that place without expecting anything in return.

I'm confident that you can now clearly distinguish between the two and determine which category your present goals fit under. Don't worry if the majority of your goals are driven by desperation; I used to have goals that were driven by desperation before I knew any better.

So how can we set goals and dreams that are motivated rather than desperate?

You don't have to make an effort to develop aspirations and dreams that are inspired by God. Naturally, we are constantly thinking about endless ideas. Children naturally have the most extravagant aspirations when it comes to their ideas and imaginations. They practically never even think about the fact that most of the time they can't do something. The only thing that separates us from children is that we have figured out how to suppress all of these creative thoughts that include the aspirations, desires, and goals we genuinely want to see come true in the world. We tend to think more about the things we can't do than the things we want to make.

When we start to worry about the thoughts we have, we immediately stop the unlimited flow of inspiration that naturally flows through us. This results in self-doubt, self-sabotage, and anxiety. Imagine the creative inspiration as a river that flows. The river always flows unless a dam or other human-made obstruction blocks it. Then, once the dam is built, we wonder why so many fish are becoming extinct, animals are vanishing, and forests are being destroyed when all we need to do is restore the river to its original state, and everything will function as nature intended.

The same holds true for our thinking and our objectives. When we are connected to our inner wisdom and inner intelligence, free from thinking, we constantly dream large, have lofty goals, and know what to do. Any thoughts regarding aspirations, goals, and wants that naturally arise are all from the divine if we simply stop thinking about them. In this way, you can "create" objectives out of inspiration rather than desperation.

"If I had infinite money, had already traveled the world, had no fear, and didn't receive any recognition for what I do, what would I do or what would I create?" is a question that helps me to focus and access the seemingly endless stream of possibilities for what I could create.

We always get responses to our questions. Our brains are unable to hear a question and not generate an answer. Therefore, whatever starts to emerge for you when you ask yourself this question without using any manual reasoning is from the divine and comes from inspiration rather than desperation.

The way the question is phrased is crucial because it gets rid of the majority of the thinking, fear, criticism, and external motivations for doing something, focusing your response on what you truly want to create (typically for no other reason than you just want to create it for fun), free from influences from the material world.

Try posing the query and see what answers you receive! When your actual dreams start to surface, don't let your thoughts cloud your judgment. You'll be amazed at what comes to the surface.

Anything is conceivable to a mind that is not constrained by thought.

Chapter Eight

POWER OF LOVE

UNCONDITIONAL LOVE

My beautiful girlfriend Anastasia taught me the meaning of unconditional love. I've spent the most of my life always asking questions. I had to understand why things were set up the way they were because otherwise, I would lose my mind. Knowing the purpose and logic behind everything prevented me from simply living.

After dating her for around a year at the time, it was only natural for me to ask Anastasia why she loved me. She kindly retorted that she had no idea why, only that she did. Then when she asked me why I loved her, I gave her a long list of explanations. It included things like her stunning smile, her endearing giggle, her kind heart, her love for her family, her intelligence, and the list could go on and on.

We've been dating for six years, and after the first time I asked her why she loved me, every few months afterward, she always responded the same way: "I don't know, I just know that I love you — a lot."

I was troubled by this for a while since I couldn't figure out why she didn't know why she loved me. She couldn't come up with even a couple of the fifty reasons I could give why I loved her. I have loved her so much throughout the years that I haven't really cared if she doesn't know. I simply accepted it and kept loving her because I was unable to stop.

It didn't occur to me why she couldn't come up with reasons why she loved me until a few months ago. I started to doubt the justifications I had for loving Anastasia. Then I experienced a life-changing epiphany.

I questioned whether I loved her more for her laugh or her passion for helping others. What would happen if she didn't laugh or help someone one day? If she doesn't act in the ways that I described as the reasons I love her, do I still love her? I came to the realization that if I make up justifications for why I love her, then it makes my affection for her dependent on those certain characteristics or behaviors, and if she doesn't exhibit them, then I don't love her. Of course, this is untrue.

I then realized that Anastasia couldn't give me a list of reasons why she loved me since we shared an unconditional love. She never gave me an explanation for her love because, if she did, it would suggest that she only felt that way when I displayed the characteristics or behaved in the ways she had imagined I should.

Her love for me transcends all "reasons" and does not stem from a sense of reciprocity; it is not contingent on how I feel or what I did. She doesn't care about me because I care about her, and she doesn't care about me because of what I can do for her. She is feeling so much love inside of herself that it is pouring out and she is giving it to me wholeheartedly.

I'm trying to express the indescribable, therefore trying to put into words how this feels and where it comes from is perhaps the toughest thing I've ever done in my life.

since of this experience, I have learned to love Anastasia without restrictions and to avoid giving her reasons or justifications why I should (since if I did, I would also be giving her reasons not to love me). Now that I've experienced it, I simply have an overflow of unrestricted love that makes it impossible for me not to love her no matter what. This unwavering love doesn't stem from motives that are outside of ourselves; rather, it comes from the limitless source that we are all descended from.

Whatever name you choose to call it—God, the Universe, or whatever—we are all connected to this unwavering, unconditional love. Our own thinking, which keeps us apart from that unwavering love, is the sole obstacle in the path of this.

CREATION WITHOUT CONDITIONS

The purest type of creation is creativity that is unconditional. We are unable to help but stand in admiration when something is produced out of unwavering love. Unconditional invention is consistently inventive, special, fresh, alluring, audacious, distinctive, and revolutionary in its own right. Because we always place restrictions on what we do or produce, there are very few people who work in this field.

For instance, once we want to earn more money, we can go and attempt to generate cash for ourselves. Because no one desires money for the sake of having money, this is conditional creation. The majority of people desire money for other purposes or the flexibility to utilize it for other things they desire.

By its very nature, this makes the work they are producing conditional. They are just making this because they want to use it for something else. Usually, when we make something for someone or something else, we don't appreciate the making process since it is always just a means to an end and never a goal in and of itself.

Because of this, we continuously feel like we are chasing, grinding, hustling, trying, and under stress and overload. Even when we succeed in our goal, we will only be able to enjoy it for a brief period of time before moving on to another objective that we must pursue because we never really found what we were seeking for.

Feelings are ultimately what we're after. To feel safe and at peace, we need more money. We desire family time because it fills us with so much love and joy. We want to pursue our passions because they make us feel internally fulfilled. We all want to experience these emotions, but we keep believing that the goal or thing we are pursuing will do so. This notion is fundamentally erroneous since feelings can never come from outside sources; they can only ever come from within. Although external factors can serve as triggers, ultimately it is we who manufacture those feelings from within ourselves.

The paradox is that when we create anything without conditions or justifications, we really experience all the wonderful emotions we desire right away.

Unconditional creation is when something is made just for the sake of being made, without any other considerations. It's not done for love, money, celebrity, or any other reason. We produce it merely out of a desire to produce it. This is abundant creation. When we work from this place, we already feel complete on the inside, and we are experiencing all the love we could ever need.

We must be in a state of non-thinking if we are to pursue unconditional creativity. The trick is to not let our minds convince us that doing something just because we want it is worthless. When we act only out of self-interest, we enter the domain of unconditional living. At this point, we encounter fluidity, oneness, and a direct link to the universe or god.

Chapter Nine

BALANCE IS THE KEY

AWARENESS OF REALITY

You've probably been able to discover serenity through non-thinking if you've been following the book's guidelines. If not, I strongly advise you to keep in mind that all of our unfavorable sentiments are a result of our thoughts. Simply becoming aware of that reality will calm your thoughts, much to how debris settles in muddy water. True serenity will be present in your life once you realize that your fears are simply thoughts and that nothing should be feared.

You can be unsure about what to do after being able to experience serenity. You may be feeling worried, anxious, or doubtful right now. Many of my clients, including myself, started to question whether they had lost their zest for life and motivation to accomplish anything. Do not be alarmed; this is all normal and a part of the awakening process.

The hardest part, which involves practicing non-thinking and stopping your negative thoughts from taking over your life, has already been taught to you.

After experiencing peace, we often suffer worry, anxiety, and doubt since we've simply let go of all we previously believed to be true about the world. Actually, the death of the individual ego occurred. The personal ego will try all in its power to reclaim control over your life if it feels threatened, which is a natural outcome.

We can never completely remove ourselves of the ego, so even when you feel at peace, you could still experience doubt, fear, and anxiety. The ego (thinking) will rise up at this time in an effort to usurp your position as ruler. But don't worry; you already know how to quickly destroy your ego (your thinking) by keeping in mind that your thoughts are the only thing responsible for your unpleasant emotions. Instead than trying to stop your thoughts from ever entering your head, the goal is to reduce the amount of time it takes you to realize that it is only your thoughts that are producing the uncomfortable feelings. We are so accustomed to thinking that it is impossible to stop it from happening.

For instance, it's in our human nature to freak out when we realize we're going to walk on a poisonous snake on our way. But when you realize that it's only a piece of rope, you see through the delusion and recognize that your fear was a result of your thoughts. As a result, you may calmly continue walking along the lovely trail. Even though we can't stop that initial reaction, all that important is that we can always remember the truth and return to our default state of serenity.

Another reason we can suffer anxiety, worry, and doubt after experiencing calm is because thinking constantly required us to expend a tremendous amount of energy. The majority of people's days are spent stressed out and thinking, which uses up a tremendous amount of energy. We return to our previous ways of putting that energy back into thinking because that is how we were conditioned. When we stop thinking, this energy you used to use to think is now "freed up" but it hasn't been directed anyplace yet. In this situation, we can direct the newly discovered energy toward our inspirational objectives. This is the remedy, and this is the intervention to stop this energy from reverting to overthinking.

So that you may focus all of your energy on it once you encounter this phenomenon, make sure that you've spent some time setting your goals out of inspiration (as opposed to desperation) and having them top of mind. Your efforts will simply serve to reinforce your negative thoughts and sentiments if you are driven by desperate aims.

Having a "activation ritual" is something that tends to be helpful for many individuals in this stage. A morning practice known as an activation ritual aids someone in entering a state of flow and non-thinking. It makes it simpler to maintain that state of non-thinking for the remainder of the day by helping you gain momentum in a positive direction as soon as you wake up. A moving thing won't stop moving. Before I realized the importance of momentum and non-thinking, I was unable to comprehend why spiritual masters and all outstanding leaders have a morning routine.

The good news is that now that you are not spending all of your energy on thinking, you can utilize this newly found energy to set new goals that will motivate and propel you into your new life of peace, joy, and love.

Chapter Ten

NOTHING IS EITHER GOOD OR BAD

THE HIGHER GOOD BEYOND GOOD AND BAD

While inner serenity does not depend on external circumstances, happiness does.

"Is it not feasible to draw only favorable circumstances into our lives? If we always have a good outlook and frame of mind, wouldn't we only attract favorable circumstances and events?"

Do you really understand what is good and bad? Do you own a whole picture? Many people have found that their greatest teachers were limitations, failure, loss, disease, or pain in any kind. It taught them to let go of distorted notions of themselves and egotistical aspirations. They gained depth, humility, and compassion as a result. It gave them more substance.

There is always a profound lesson hidden within anything bad that happens to you, even though you might not realize it at the moment. Even a brief sickness or accident might make you realize what is really important in life and what isn't.

Conditions are always favorable when viewed from a higher perspective. They are neither good nor negative, to be more specific. They exist as they do. There is no longer "good" or "bad" in your life when you live in total acceptance of what is, which is the only sane way to live. There is only a higher good, which encompasses everything deemed "bad." But when viewed through the lens of the mind, there is good and terrible, like and dislike, and love and hate. As a result, it is stated in the Book of Genesis that once Adam and Eve "ate of the tree of the knowledge of good and evil," they were no longer permitted to live in "paradise."

HOW WE PERCEIVE THINGS

William Shakespeare said: "There is nothing either good or bad but thinking makes it so."

An average piano has 88 keys. We don't point out particular keys on a piano and declare them to be "wrong" just for the sake of doing so. We only consider a key to be "wrong" if we believe someone is playing a particular song and strikes an unrelated key.

However, there are no incorrect keys on a piano by nature. There are only a few keys and notes that, when played consecutively, provide a more or less pleasing sound.

There are no "wrong" decisions in life, just as there are no wrong piano notes. Only our thoughts can elicit positive or negative emotions in us. We create dualism and conditions in our lives when we categorize things as either good or terrible. These factors then affect how we feel.

For instance, if we feel that the opposing political parties are wrong or bad, this might breed resentment and a slew of unfavorable feelings within us.

of the other hand, if we consider that there are no essentially "wrong" parties and that different political parties are really like the many keys of a piano, we allow ourselves to enjoy love, joy, and serenity in the present. We have the chance to increase our awareness of the fundamental essence of existence when we start to see new, alternate viewpoints.

It is comparable to trekking up a mountain and stopping at strategic locations to take in the breathtaking scenery. There are no "wrong" places to stop, pause, and admire the beauty of nature, but by being open to all potential places we can stand, we can view the scene from angles we haven't seen before.

Search for truth rather than what is right or wrong, good or terrible in the world. Look for the truth in what is immediately in front of you rather than trying to prove that we are right and they are wrong, or that they are superior and we are worse. I would only add the caveat that a lot of individuals do believe what they perceive to be the truth. Without this deeper comprehension of life, the majority of what we believe is not reality, despite the fact that it may appear to be so.

The real truth is objective. It is not universal truth if it is "true" for one person but not another. Consider what holds true for every aware person on the earth, regardless of who they are, where they are from, or what their history is. That is the real truth, and there you will discover everything you have been looking for. Never attempt to hunt for this outside of yourself; it can only be found in the depths of your existence.

When faced with something that can make you feel bad, look within to discover the universal truth that lies at the heart of your spirit. You will search for all of eternity and never discover the solution if you try to locate the answers outside or try to investigate external causes for the base of why you feel this way.

Negative feelings are a sign of miscommunication. When we experience negative emotions, it indicates that we are considering what we are feeling. We have just forgotten at this point how our experiences came about and that our bad feelings are a result of our thoughts.

All you need to do is keep in mind that our feelings are primarily caused by our thoughts. Don't oppose the thought once you become aware of this. Simply recognize that your thoughts are what are making you feel bad, accept it with love, and watch it gently go away. You'll quickly get back to your natural condition of joy, love, and calm.

Chapter Eleven

WHAT TO DO WITHOUT THINKING?

THE TRUTH THAT IS WITHIN YOU

We established in the prior chapter that neither right nor wrong exists in the real world. This chapter will expand on the previous one by explaining how to act without having to consciously decide what to do.

Just as there are no wrong keys on a piano, there are no bad choices we may make; yet, certain choices or "keys" are more pleasurable than others. The burden of having to "make the right choice" is greatly lessened when we accept that there is no such thing.

To avoid overthinking, we prefer to go with our gut instincts. Anxiety and irritation set in when we try to think it through, analyze it, develop a list of benefits and disadvantages, and get input from everyone (including our pets). The vast majority of the time, we instinctively know the best course of action to take. The term "intuition" or "inner wisdom" is commonly used to describe this. What we do is try to corroborate our gut feelings with evidence from the outside world, and this is when the majority of our negative emotions start to bubble to the surface and wreak havoc on our state of mind.

What you really want to do, only you can decide. Besides myself, nobody else knows this. Mentors and coaches are there to support you along the path, but the finest among them will encourage you to trust your gut and search inward for the answer (because you are the only one who truly knows the truth). Because of this, many of us have felt the pangs of regret after making a decision that went against our better judgment because we heeded the advise of others instead of our own intuition.

If you follow your gut, you'll know exactly where you should go and what you should do at any given time. It's like having an internal GPS that can alert you to roadblocks and direct you to alternate routes in real time. Our internal navigation system will unfailingly lead us to our desired destination; what is unpredictable is the specific route it will take us along. Your GPS will get you there no matter what happens on the way, and there are limitless ways that could go wrong.

Take Note: In virtually all cases, our intuition will not be validated by society until after the fact. Looking outside for validation of what you already know to be true is futile since you will almost always encounter resistance and conflicting advice.

Don't bother searching elsewhere for the solutions. Listen to your gut, your inner voice, your spiritual guides, and the Universe/God. When you do this, miraculous things will start to happen in your life that you never thought possible. Those who have the conviction and fortitude to do so will experience the fullness of life and all its wonders for the first time.

What then allows us to act without deliberate consideration?

Most of us are aware of the proper course of action, but we are too timid to take it. For instance, most of us know exactly what to do if we want to reduce weight. Getting thin isn't some secret formula encoded in hieroglyphics. Most of us are aware that if we burn more calories than we take in through exercise and proper eating, we will experience weight loss. If you want to succeed at anything in life, chances are you already know what to do, but you're either too afraid to try or don't think you're good enough to succeed.

The first thing to do is to accept the fact that you do know what to do; you just aren't doing it because of doubt or fear. Trust your inner wisdom (Infinite Intelligence) that it will give you the solutions you need if you have no fear or self-doubt about the circumstance but yet see that you don't know what to do. Since we have access to a limitless store of ideas, there is never a time when you will be at a loss for what to do next. Our own way of thinking is the only thing preventing us from tapping into this pool of information.

A wise man once said, "Whether you think you can or can't, you're right." That wise man was Henry Ford. If we go about our days with an attitude of "I can't," we immediately close ourselves off to the infinite opportunities that exist right now. But when we let go of the mental brake and see that it's only our thinking that's holding us back, we return to our natural condition of abundance and limitless possibilities, and we may get any response we need at that same time.

In other words, trust that you know what you need to know, and if you don't, trust that you can.

If you have faith in your own ability to know, you'll never be without the information you require. Rely on your own judgment and gut feelings. If you have faith in it, it will be there for you whenever you need it, as it has been and always has been.

Chapter Twelfth

HOW TO FOLLOW YOUR INTUITION

THE DIVINE CONNECTION

In a previous chapter, we discussed how thinking is not necessary for us to thrive in the world and that the best way to do so is to stop thinking. Oneness with everything around us and a direct connection define the condition of flow. We can also argue that state is one in which we are in direct touch and alignment with God/Universe/ Infinite Intelligence because there is no separation when we are in that condition.

Thinking breaks down our spiritual connection, which results in the unpleasant emotions that many of us experience on a daily basis, such as stress, frustration, wrath, resentment, and sadness. Because of this, some religions define Hell as being totally cut off from God.

In this book, I'll refer to flow as non-thinking, but I'll use it interchangeably from now on for the purpose of simplicity. This non-thinking condition also entails a direct relationship with Infinite Intelligence.

Many people believe that the only time we may be in a state of non-thinking or flow is when we are engaged in an activity we love. This is not at all the case. At any time, we are capable of becoming non-thinking. Only in the present moment can we truly be in a state of non-thinking. Since we can only see reality in the here and now, thinking implies that we are either in the past or future, neither of which exist. The truth can only be discovered in the present time. This is why all spiritual teachers and leaders consistently emphasize the importance of mindfulness, meditation, and prayer. When Moses asks God her name in the Bible, God simply responds, "I am," not "I was" or "I will be" (because those things don't exist). All of these concepts—God, truth, the Universe, freedom, peace, joy, and love—can only be discovered and so experienced in the present.

When you trust yourself and believe you always have the inner wisdom needed to help lead you through everything in life, you are following your intuition. This is a non-thinking or flow state.

Let's look at how we may apply this idea to our daily lives and make it practical. What does it mean to listen to your intuition and inner guidance, and how can we achieve that?

When you listen to your intuition, you are fully connected to something bigger than your individual self. You are in a state of flow where you are not thinking and are in close contact with God. In this state, infinite intelligence directs you and you always know what to do without having to think about it. When we are in this state, we nearly appear to be doing nothing because we have lost our sense of self and have united with life. When we're in this mindset, miracles like sudden business agreements, individuals appearing at the perfect moment, money arriving right when we need it, connections we were hoping for spontaneously falling into our laps, and life seeming almost magical happen. Because there is no sense of time, it appears to distort and bend around us. Then we go on to accomplish more in a few days than other people do in a month. In this state, sentiments of plenty, love, joy, peace, harmony, and thankfulness are unavoidable and inseparable.

Each and every one of us has felt this way at some point in the past. Despite the fact that many people have encountered this phenomenon, relatively few are able to sustain it over long periods of time. The fundamental cause is that most people revert to thinking and assume they must "figure it out" on their own. We stop having this ability to enact miraculous situations and events once we start thinking.

The truth is that we don't need to know everything and that we don't even need to try to figure it all out. How is it possible for our finite minds to comprehend the entire world and attempt to bend it to our will?

Problems only arise when we believe our knowledge exceeds that of God.

FAITH IN OUR INNER WISDOM

The good news is that neither of us need to think nor need to know more than She does. People who are most prosperous, happy, and successful typically credit luck or a higher power for their accomplishment when you ask them how they did it. Instead of attributing their accomplishment to pure determination and force, these people attribute it to believing in something bigger than themselves.

There are so many aspects of life that are totally outside our control, and we actually only have a very limited amount of control over those aspects. This is not to say we give up because we have no control over our life; quite the contrary. When we come to terms with the fact that we don't have to exert our will or try to make things go our way, we are liberated from anguish, pain, and frustration and start to lapse into a condition of non-thinking in which everything just happens for us rather than to us. We start to realize that everything in our lives was put exactly where it needed to be in order for us to become who we are today. If anything in our lives had been different, we would not have what we have now. For us to be in the position we are now, countless minute details and events had to be carefully planned. That would be impossible and pointless to plan, yet here we are. The marvel of life is this.

I want to emphasize a qualification to our previous assertion that we do not have to exercise personal control over the events in our lives. While it is true that we have no control over everything that occurs in our life, we do have power over how we choose to think, which is the main source of all of our issues and unfavorable feelings. We have the choice to alter how we feel and how we perceive life whenever we want. By making the decision to let go of our thinking, we can choose to be happy. Isn't that really what matters in the end? The actual indicator of success, joy, and contentment is how we feel on the inside, not what we possess.

The other thing I wanted to mention is that even while there are many things we can't control, we do have some influence over what we want out of life, but not always the how. Because we have access to infinite intelligence and the gift of imagination, for instance, we are able to create anything we desire in life. This is a wonderful blessing, but when we believe that we must figure out the details in order to make it happen, things might turn sour. At this stage, the majority of individuals either give up or continue on the path of using force to try to revive it while enduring daily suffering. This is the reason why many people think we must toil and suffer in order to achieve our goals in life. Simply said, that is untrue. It only holds true if we believe we must figure out the "how" to achieve our goals in life. It is our responsibility to determine what we want, not how to acquire it. The universe will ultimately decide how. This is the best-case situation since there are an endless number of methods to achieve your goals in life, making it pointless for our limited minds to try to figure it out.

We only suffer when we make an effort to understand everything, but we don't have to. This is the time to rely on our inner guidance and intuition to guide us just what to do right now to create our desires. There's no need to attempt to anticipate everything. Our role is to visualize what we want and enter a condition of non-thought. This permits us to connect with our infinite intelligence (God), who will then disclose the solutions to us at the precise moment we need them.

We can't see the way forward until we start walking. There will never be a day when we can look ahead and see the full path lighted. That would utterly disprove the requirement for faith, which is why having faith and belief in something is crucial when manifesting it.

We can only have complete, unwavering faith in the Universe's orchestration of how what we wish to produce will come to us if we fully trust it to do so. Although it might not happen on our timeline or in the way we want it to, we can always achieve our goals in life.

Actually, we are always being spoken to by our inner wisdom and intuition (God). Do you have a little voice within that always tells you what to do? Perhaps you want to quit your job, ask someone out, or make up with someone you've been estranged from. You know what you need to do when you get that gut feeling. Have you ever wished you had acted immediately when your instincts urged you to? Have you ever had a gut feeling to act on something even if you couldn't explain why, and as a result, fantastic things transpired? You have instincts about that.

Although we do experience our intuition as thoughts, keep in mind that, as we covered in a previous chapter, there is a significant distinction between thoughts and thinking. By their very nature, thoughts are divine and seem to appear out of thin air. On the other hand, thinking is a manual, exhausting endeavor that we make for ourselves; it feels quite weighty and often evokes negative emotions. There is a feeling of knowingness when you are experiencing divine thoughts from Infinite Intelligence. It is accurate, and you just know in your heart that it is. Your intuition will virtually never seem logical or sensible, but we want that because we don't want it to be predictable, so we want it to appear that way. It wouldn't be miraculous or include the limitless possibilities of the Universe, which are all spontaneous by their very nature, if it were predictable.

Be prepared for the fact that your intuition will nearly always conflict with your logical, reasoning intellect. It will suggest to you that you should strike up a conversation with this stranger in the coffee shop, which results in a lovely friendship, or that you should call a friend on the spur of the moment, where you discover that they truly needed someone to be there for them during a trying time. It will advise you to embrace your divine gift, live it, and present yourself to the world as a truth-teller. It will subtly encourage you to go after what you really want in life rather than what other people think you ought to want. These are only a few of the countless ways it will talk to you, and when you listen to it, it will always work wonders and bring you abundance that is beyond your wildest dreams.

If intuition always knows what to do and provides prosperity anytime it is followed, then why don't more people follow it? Fear.

It might be quite intimidating or frightening to listen to our intuition. This is so because the realm of the unknown is where our intuition resides. To put it another way, our intuition is spiritual and works in the area of limitless potential, which is by definition an area of uncertainty.

Because we cannot foretell what might occur, people have a natural aversion to the unknown. We may only start to explore the endless possibilities that life can offer us when we take a step into the unknown. This is why when we trust our intuition, miraculous occurrences and miracles occur. We are actually entering a realm of limitless potential.

We just need to understand the "what" of what we wish to create; the "how" is not necessary.

You can only access this realm of miracles by ceasing to think. If we think, we are quickly expelled from the present moment and go into a condition of worry, anxiety, and sorrow. Based on the past, our thinking will attempt to forecast potential outcomes. Because of this, most people continue to receive the same things.

They mistakenly fail to see that they must enter the condition of non-thinking and listen to their intuition in order to venture into the unknown. Instead, they attempt to utilize their limited personal mind to create something they have never experienced before. In the universe of endless possibilities, we can only ever create something we have never seen or experienced, and the only way to do that is to venture into the unknown.

Steve Jobs said: "You can't connect the dots looking forward; you can only connect them looking backwards. So you have to trust that the dots will somehow connect in your future."

In conclusion, you can access your intuition by entering a state of non-thinking since it always knows what you need to accomplish right now. Your own mind will go into overdrive because you're entering the realm of limitless potential (the unknown), but if you keep in mind that fear is simply thinking, the fear will go, and the courage you need to follow your intuition will come to you spontaneously.

You must have faith in your inner wisdom (God) in this moment to lead you through life even when you are unsure of what will happen next; yet, that is the adventure and joy of it. The only way to create what you desire in life, if you don't already have it, is also in the unknown. To gain what you don't have, you must do what you haven't done. It's not as if you'll constantly feel afraid while you're acting on intuition.

Only when you are actively thinking about dread is there any terror. The illusion will dissolve once you confront the fear and realize that it is only your thoughts that are responsible for those feelings, and you will return to a state of serenity, joy, and unadulterated love. You should remain in this area because it will help you generate the good feelings necessary to manifest anything you can possibly envision for yourself.

Chapter Thirteen

CREATING A MIRACLE SPACE

THE LAW OF VOID

We come to understand that everything originates from nothing as we study the universe and quantum physics. The Great Nothingness is what the great spiritual gurus refer to as. There must be space before there can be creation. We can say the same about our own thinking. You must first make room in your mind so that you can acquire fresh insights that have the power to transform your life if you want to create something new, such as new thoughts. Similar to the teacup, if your mind is entirely filled with outdated ideas, no new ideas will be able to enter in and bring about the desired change.

Through non-thinking, we can create this space. We quickly make room in our minds for fresh ideas to arrive once we stop making arduous efforts to think. Another effective strategy for clearing our brains is to ask questions that contradict our preconceived notions.

In this void zone, all the magic takes place. For instance, the top athletes understand the necessity for an equally rigorous period of recovery after intense training sessions in order to maintain peak performance. They recover, gain muscle, and get stronger during this period of rest. Everything they desired from the workout manifests in the space they give themselves during rest.

Thomas Edison would fall asleep in his chair with a steel ball in each hand when he was faced with a particularly difficult task. He would eventually fall asleep for a long enough period of time that when the ball would fall, he would be awakened, and an answer to his problem would suddenly come to him. Everything starts from nothing, and Edison recognized this idea. He allowed room for new ideas to enter his mind rather than making an effort to solve problems using his pre-existing style of thinking. He was aware that holding onto outdated ideas would not help him find a solution to his problems.

"We can't use the same level of consciousness we had when we created them to solve problems." Einstein, Albert

Like Edison, Einstein displayed a variety of odd, cryptic behaviors yet had a similar grasp of how to organize space. Einstein would take a break from solving a challenging issue to play the violin. While he was playing, the answer would appear out of nowhere, and he would suddenly have the answer to his dilemma. Through non-thinking, Einstein made room in his mind so that he might receive heavenly downloads from the universe.

We don't need to try to solve every puzzle. What makes us believe that we must exert ourselves in order to create the biggest discoveries in history when even the people we regard as geniuses didn't? We have a common source with them and are not distinct from them. We can also gain insights into any problem we're encountering with the right understanding. We can always have an entirely different experience of life by simply having a different thinking, an insight, or an idea.

The procedure for getting divine downloads when you're faced with a challenge is as follows:

1. Recognize that all bad emotions stem from your thoughts.

2. Clear some space in your mind by letting go of any manual reasoning, and have complete faith that your inner wisdom—God, the universe, or infinite intelligence—will provide the solution. Also give up the way and time that the solution will come to you.

3. Pay attention to any emotions that surface as you give up and amplify any sensations of love, peace, and joy. If you approach your situation with love, the solution will reveal itself to you.

It's advantageous if it seems nearly overly straightforward. Truth is always straightforward. Even the most accomplished spiritual masters occasionally face difficulties, despite the fact that it may seem simple. Because it happens all the time, it doesn't matter when we become stuck in our thoughts; what matters is what we do when we do. You can remain free as long as you keep in mind that we can never feel anything other than what we are thinking about, and that thinking is the source of all of our pain.

Chapter Fourteen

LIVING IN THE FLOW-STATE

You'll undoubtedly find some obstacles on your path, so I'd want to discuss some of those possible problems now to make it a little bit simpler for you when you do.

You'll have a great time without having many worries, stresses, or troubles in your life once you start living in the flow-state. Many of them will just disappear before your eyes because, when you stop seeing something as a problem, it ceases to be one for you. It will feel alien to you because you have never experienced this level of tranquility and quiet in your life.

Because unfamiliarity connotes uncertainty, humans by nature dislike it. Ironically, most people start to suspect that something is amiss about this time since they have felt so content and at peace for the majority of the day. Many believe that they are less productive, have lost their "edge," or are simply becoming lazy. It's your brain's attempt to start thinking again to give the impression of "safety" it wants to feel, which is far from the truth. The truth is that when we are content and not thinking, we are at our most productive as people. When we are experiencing absolute bliss, time seems to pass quickly. Work is simpler, we work more effectively, people are drawn to us, we attract a lot more abundance, and miracles start happening out of nowhere. You only need to experience these things for a brief period of time in order to never want to return to thinking.

At this point, having trust that everything will turn out alright becomes of the biggest significance. Recognize that the universe is on your side and not against you. think everything happens for a purpose and that life is full of opportunities for growth rather than failures. Because there is only opportunity for anything to be different from the life we currently lead in the unknown, we must have trust in it. All possibilities, including all you could possibly want in life, reside in the unknown. It is unthinkable that your life won't change once you have the fortitude to take the plunge into the unknown and to lose your fear of it.

If you start to worry that something is wrong because you feel so at peace and satisfied, remember that this is just your mind trying to get you to think again. The best salesperson you have is your mind, and it knows just what to say to entice you back into its damaging thought patterns. You have the decision right now to either return to your old patterns of psychological suffering and familiar sorrow or to have confidence in the unknowable and stay in the state of happiness, peace, and love. Either we can choose to remain constrained and unhappy in the known, or we can choose to be free and joyful in the unknown.

It's totally fine if you start to think again. Do not punish yourself for it. Don't feel bad about what happened. Punishing yourself won't help because it will just reinforce the way you believe. Realize that thinking is entirely human. All you need to do to return to a condition of peace, joy, and love is to recognize when you are suffering and realize that it is your thoughts that are to blame. If you let it, the transition can take place effortlessly and without any suffering.

Chapter Fifteen

NOW WHAT?

Even if the book is now finished, your new existence is just getting started. Peace, love, and joy, which come from a state of non-thinking, are always just one thought away. This is the only reason for hope you will ever need when times are difficult, so keep it in mind and near to your heart. I said at the outset that you wouldn't be the same person you were before reading this book. If you approached this book with the aim of reading it with an open and willing mind, you have already gleaned a great deal of knowledge that has fundamentally altered the way you view the world, and as a result, you are not the same person you were before. You cannot unsee anything after you have gained new insight into it. Your consciousness cannot contract once it has expanded. Even though we may occasionally forget this and suffer when we start thinking again, as soon as we do, we become aware that we are the ever-expanding awareness of life itself and experience love, serenity, and joy in the moment.

If you feel as though this is too straightforward and cannot possibly be all there is, this is merely your mind forcing you to reconsider. The truth is straightforward and always will be. Any attempt to make things deep and complicated will only lead you further from the truth. The truth is something you know and feel in your heart and soul, not something you think. Pay attention to the still, inner wisdom that understands everything. Let it be your life's compass. When we follow our soul, we are most content. The world will always try to convince us that we are lacking something or that we don't have what we want. You'll be inundated with people's opinions, assessments, and suggestions all the time. Recognize that they are merely distracted by their thoughts and express your gratitude for their concern, but resist the temptation to believe that you require any of it. You already possess everything you could possible need and want. You already possess everything of the love, happiness, tranquility, and contentment you could possibly desire. Only when we lose sight of that reality and become preoccupied with our thoughts do we fail to notice it.

Let go of any thoughts that may arise as you stay in this condition of absolute tranquility. More miracles will appear in your life if you remain in this area for a longer period of time. You can go out and tell everyone you encounter this message, but you won't even need to since they will see something entirely different in you. They'll start wondering why and how because you'll be radiant, beaming, and radiating nothing but love and delight. You now possess all the knowledge required to put an end to your own psychological suffering and manifest the constant, attainable state of peace, love, and joy. It's likely that you have already felt the joy of understanding and becoming this.

The fact that you chose to read this book and that we are able to share our trip here with one another are not at all coincidences. The number of divine intercessions that have to occur for us to be present together at this time never ceases to astound me. The fact that you have trusted me to help you navigate this incredibly wonderful experience we call life is both humbling and a tremendous blessing.

I do have one last request before we wrap off this chapter. It would be a great honor if you could spend 60 seconds reviewing this book on Amazon if you found it to be informative or helpful. I would sincerely appreciate hearing about your ideas, perceptions, criticisms, personal journey, and anything in between. Your brief comments there will help disseminate this message to countless people who are seeking the same solutions as you are and could even save someone's life (after all, who doesn't check Amazon reviews before making a purchase?).

P.S. There will be a summary and how-to guides for much of what is discussed in this book in the following few pages.

SUMMARY OF STOP OVERTHINKING: Calm Your Emotions, Manage Stress, Reduce Anxiety and Find Yourself

CONCLUSION

The source of all misery is thought.

There is no alternative explanation for why we experience negative feelings than the fact that our own thoughts are to blame. Since our mind is the source of everything, solving problems is quite straightforward. We may let go of it and return to our natural state of peace, love, and joy once we become aware that our thoughts are what are causing how we feel. When we let go of our thoughts, we make room for all the good feelings we wish to experience to come to the surface. Our perception of reality, which is a product of our own thinking, is what we actually live in.

Instead of being a result of our experiences, thinking is their CAUSE.

Our thoughts are not actual facts.

We can only be controlled by our thoughts if we accept them as true. Give up your faith in the idea that you can stop experiencing pain.

Our feelings serve as immediate feedback and a natural internal guiding system that tells us whether we are fully aware of the truth or whether we are in need of more education. Feelings are a call to expand our knowledge of reality. When we are not thinking, we are in flow.

When we are not thinking, there is no distinction between us and the universe or all of life. We only shut ourselves off from Source and feel distinct from everything when we think (this is the emergence of the ego).

Thoughts and thinking are two distinct concepts. Thinking is a verb that demands our manual labor, which is painful. Nouns are things that do not originate in us but rather are divine downloads from the cosmos.

Because it is a biological reaction to survive, we suppose. Our minds simply think in order to keep us alive; it does not assist in our development. It doesn't care about our happiness; it only cares about our safety and survival. Because it makes us feel bad, thinking keeps us from becoming our Highest Selves and keeps us from pursuing our genuine callings.

We can only think about things we have personally experienced. Simply choose to listen to Infinite Intelligence rather than your finite intellect if you want to gain insights, creativity, and knowledge that are greater than what your current self is capable of receiving. If we allow it to be, this limitless wellspring of truth is accessible to everyone at all times.

Everything in the cosmos is made of energy, which is known as universal intelligence or mind. We are made of it, and it is the origin of all things that existed before taking on physical form. There is a sensation associated with this energy, and that feeling is one of love, peace, joy, connection, and wellbeing. When we stop thinking, we automatically revert to this state, which is also our default state.

When we let go of our thinking, we have access to fresh concepts, ideas, and insights—even if we have never encountered them before—because we are all constantly connected to the same source of Infinite Intelligence. These insights are constantly available to us, and the more we trust our intuition and this Infinite Intelligence, the more we will get them. Our natural states as humans are those of peace, love, joy, and all other positive emotions. We are only pulled out of that natural condition when we start thinking. When we let go of our thoughts, we return to our natural state of being and effortlessly enjoy all good emotions.

We can always experience a greater sense of love that arises from a condition of non-thinking, and we are always just one thought or insight away from doing so.

Our minds are naturally clear and in this state by default. Things only seem different when we are preoccupied with our thoughts. When we stop thinking, we revert to our "factory default" state of tranquility, love, and happiness.

Nobody or everything in the universe is intrinsically flawed, but our way of thinking will lead us to believe that they are. Because you are not broken, you do not need to be mended. There is only one thing you need to understand and keep in mind: thinking is what leads to all of our pain. Regarding your mindset, there is nothing you need to do. You only need to change how you view thought to get back to the real you, which transcends thought, the physical body, and all of your preconceived notions. When you stop thinking, you merge with Infinite Intelligence and can experience an endless supply of love, serenity, and joy since that is your actual nature and it is always there for you to experience.

Infinite Intelligence makes room for you when you create space for it. It trusts you more the more you trust it. There is no limit to how much room you may create for it. Your life will change when you put an emphasis on creating room in your life and in your thinking for Infinite Intelligence to manifest.

HOW TO STOP THINKING: A GUIDE

Eliminate anything that could increase your propensity for thought or send you into flight or fight mode.

As many activities and items in your life that don't thrill or inspire you should be eliminated.

Make an environment that encourages you to stop thinking.

Make up a morning ritual to help you wake up peacefully and without thinking. Take advantage of this area to learn life lessons from infinite intelligence.

Make time in your schedule so that you can unwind, unwind, and go back to not thinking. Make a list of daily activities that will help you do this. It could be soothing activities like blogging, walking, meditating, playing with your pets, sleeping, practicing yoga, or anything else.

A Plan for Quitting Thinking

1. Recognize that thinking—or at least the fundamental nature of thinking—is the source of all pain.
Recognize that you are thinking if you are hurting.
Understand the distinction between thinking and thoughts. Don't look for the root reason; the root cause is thinking.

2. Make room for persistently pessimistic thinking
Recognize them for who they are and accept them as they are.
Recognize that although these sensations are held in a sacred space within of you, you are not the feelings.
Don't be frightened to think alone, and have the bravery to let your thoughts per-

meate your brain.

Accept it and observe that thought merely seeks recognition.

Recognize that you can only be affected by negative thoughts if you give them credence.

You may look beyond the feelings to find the reality underlying it all if you give them permission to exist in your consciousness and don't fight the feelings.

Every emotion carries a kernel of reality that will heighten your consciousness and let you live life to the fullest.

3. After acknowledging the thought, let it time to pass and then just be without clinging to anything. Natural feelings of joy, love, and tranquility will naturally surface. Take time to experience these feelings as they arise. Go back to step one and repeat it if the bad feeling still exists till you can find some calm.

Potential Difficulties

1. Reticence to let go of thought because you believe it is what brought you here.

While this is true, you must understand that your current course of action will not take you there. You'll need to take alternative action if you want to escape the cycle of misery and the same negative behaviors that keep reoccurring in your life. The definition of insanity is repeating an action while hoping for a different outcome. The true query is whether or not you desire happiness. You can take the leap of faith into non-thinking if you realize that thinking is the source of all of your misery and you don't want to be unhappy any longer.

2. Insufficient faith

You must first think that it is conceivable for there to even be a potential that there could be a life full with joy, serenity, and love every single day. A person must also think that the life force that has been looking after them their entire lives (the Universe/God) is a part of something far bigger. The only way we can relinquish our manual efforts and have complete serenity in our lives as opposed to worrying about everything is to have confidence in something that is far bigger than we are without being able to fully comprehend it with our finite intellect.

3. Fear

When it comes to having faith in the Universe, which is also the unknown, fear is a perfectly reasonable emotion. This is a fantastic sign because fear is a sign that something is highly essential to us. Deep down, you know that this is true: everything we could ever want is on the other side of fear. Fear itself is the hurdle we need to jump in order to achieve what we want. The only way out is through looking deeply within yourself and realizing that you will always be fine. That although this fear cannot and will not harm you, if you do not face it, it will kill all of your dreams. The main source of terror is thought. Fear does not exist if you do not think. Follow the steps in the thinking-stopping framework to get over your fear and discover what a limitless life is like.

How To Recognize When You Are In A State Of Non-Thinking

You will feel every happy emotion your mind can imagine, including total serenity, love, joy, passion, excitement, inspiration, and happiness, if you aren't thinking. You'll experience a state of flow. You'll become disoriented and maybe lose your sense of self. You'll experience being "one" with life. You can tell you are not thinking when this happens.

Reflection Questions

How much did you think today, from 1 to 10? What proportion of your day was spent in fight-or-flight mode (1 being low, 10 being high)? How much time was spent in a peaceful, relaxed state?

How To Create A Non-Thinking Environment: A Guide

Your surroundings can either encourage and promote thinking or they might increase your propensity for thinking.

Even if we design our reality from the inside out, the environment still frequently has an impact on us. It is crucial to create a space that supports non-thinking because we cannot yet fully separate from this 3D world because we are spiritual beings residing in a physical universe. Eliminating distractions is preferable to attempting to do more in order to be more productive.

Similar to this, it will be much simpler for us to maintain a tranquil state of non-thinking if we get rid of many of the things we are aware of causing us to relapse. Keep in mind that it won't be sustainable to change your environment rather than yourself. To design a lovely life you love to live, you will need to carefully combine the two.

Framework For Removing Thought-Provoking Factors

1.   Conduct an audit to identify the factors that may increase your propensity for pondering, then develop a list of them.

A. Compose a list of all the ideas that occur to mind. Using your intuition and your body's innate ability to sense energy can assist in determining if a certain element in your environment will benefit or harm you. If you're calm and at ease, the solution will be clear.

B. If you're having difficulties coming up with ideas, try to recall what tends to make you anxious, trigger your fight-or-flight response, or cause you to overthink. Anything that triggers a sense of survival will prevent you from continuing to be non-thinking.

C. If it's still hard for you to think clearly, keep a notebook as you go about your week and jot down anything that makes you feel like you need to run or hide. By the end of the week, you'll have a nice list.

2. Classify anything you noted down into appropriate groups. A. Here are a few categories to consider

I. Physical Fitness

What substances (such as anxiety, stress, and overthinking) can increase your risk of having a fight-or-flight response when you put them into your body? foods, drinks, and stimulants, etc.

What aspects of your physical environment can increase your risk of having a fight-or-flight response (anxiety, stress, overthinking)?

II. Digital Environment

What images, sounds, or videos on your phone, computer, or TV might increase your risk of having a fight-or-flight reaction (anxiety, tension, or overthinking)?

III. Use of digital devices

What media or content do you often consume that may increase your risk of having a fight-or-flight reaction (anxiety, tension, or overthinking)?

3. After categorizing everything, rearrange your list and start rating the elements according to how much each one affects you.

4. Pick the top items from each list, and then make an action item outlining what you're going to do to get rid of them from your surroundings. Only pick things that you can handle and get rid of without making yourself more prone to stress (which would negate the exercise's objective). Start by getting used to the adjustments and seeing their effects, then start getting rid of other things.

Setting Up A Non-Thinking Environment: A Framework

Make a list of all the practices and strategies that help you unwind, be at peace, and stop thinking. Sort the items on your list into categories, and they could include activities like exercise, meditation, listening to a particular genre of music, being in a particular place, etc.

1. Illustrations Of Categories I. Physical Health a. What foods do you consume that make you feel physically well, energized for a long time, and at peace?

What elements of your physical environment contribute to your sense of alignment with your divine self? What features on your phone, computer, or TV make you feel in tune with your divine self? III. Digital Environment a.

What media or information do you consume that helps you feel in alignment with your highest self?

2. Determine which objects in each category have the greatest and least significant effects on your ability to enter and maintain a state of non-thinking.

3. Select the most important elements from each list, then make an action plan for how you will apply each one to your daily life. Avoid taking on too much at once because it might be stressful. For the time being, only take on what you can handle; once you've gotten the hang of it, you can add more.

4. Establish a morning ritual or activation ritual to assist you achieve a state of non-thinking and align with your highest self. Make a plan for the ideal morning routine that you can implement right away. Don't overwhelm yourself; start small. Make sure you have time to dedicate to spiritual practices that will help you connect with infinite intelligence, such as yoga, meditation, or creating space.

5. Your day's progress will be influenced by how you start it. By checking your phone, emails, and to-do list first thing in the morning, you're setting yourself up for a stressed, "fight or flight" mindset that will last the rest of the day.

6. It will be much harder to become distracted by outside factors that can cause you to relapse back into thinking and tension if you start your day in a calm condition and follow a pattern that gets you into a state of non-thinking. The greatest spiritual masters all have morning rituals or habits of some form because of this.

A Plan for Integrating Non-Thinking Into Your Work

1. Make a note of the tasks you perform at work that make you feel drained of energy – tasks you dislike performing or that make you feel like your workload is heavy in general.

2. making a list of the activities you engage in at work that inspire you, making you feel energised, alive, and light.

3. Review your entire list and rate each activity on a scale of 1 to 10, with 1 being the most depleting on your energy and 10 making you feel the most alive and inspired.

4. Every week, cut one to three items from your list of activities that sap your energy and focus more on the nine and ten activities.

5. The objective is to reach a point where you spend 80% of your working hours on tasks that rate a 9 or 10.

A Manual For Breaking Bad Habits and Behaviours

You'll quickly learn that you'll become aware of a lot of bad, destructive behaviors you may have that keep making you more vulnerable to pain as you start to make more space and start thinking less. This is perfectly OK. Do not criticize yourself because doing so will just make the situation worse. Here is a more thorough guide that will assist you in kicking any bad habits:

1.   Identify the behavior you want to modify and make sure it's something you really want to do. Recognize that in order to alter your situation and break the cycle of suffering, you will need to let go of the beliefs you still hold onto and modify them. There is no point in moving forward if you don't want to alter it, but if you do, let's start the process of letting go.

2. Describe in minute, exact detail what occurs when this conduct occurs (how frequently, when, etc.). Give every last detail.

3. In the instant before you start the activity, how are you feeling? What emotion causes the behavior to occur? Be truthful to yourself.

4. What specific thought processes are present? What are you telling yourself at the time this occurs? Give full details of it.

5. What ideas do you hold about this behavior? What inferences have you drawn that make you feel you MUST engage in this behavior or action?

6. How do you feel after having that thought?

7. If you don't engage in the behavior, what do you think will happen? Or, to put it another way, what do you think will happen if you don't do the thing?

8. Is it CERTAINLY TRUE that it will occur if you don't act in a certain way?

9. Do you realize how harmful this way of thinking is and how much suffering it causes you?

10. Are you ready to let rid of this way of thinking and acting right now?

11. Speak with your highest self and inner wisdom. What message is it trying to

convey? What is it attempting to teach you? How is it advising you to get your life back in balance? How is it currently urging you to develop? Make room and wait for a revelation from Infinite Intelligence about the real reason you wish to change.

12. Once you get the knowledge, give yourself permission to truly experience the freedom, tranquility, and joy. Feel the strain being removed from your shoulders. If you physically and energetically feel lighter and if you no longer perceive the action or habit in the same way, you know you done it correctly. Allow yourself to completely lose yourself in the emotion of profound thankfulness.

13. Keep a journal of your experience and any insights you have so you have a record of these miracles in your life.

How to Respond If the Feeling Resurfaces

Repeat these steps until you come to a realization or have a breakthrough that fundamentally alters the way you view life.